The Rise with Love:
Eric Walton in Rare Art Form

Eric Walton

Copyright © 2013, 2014, 2016 Eric Walton

All rights reserved.

ISBN: 1494289342

ISBN-13: 978-1494289348

The Album Credits

The Rise with Love: Eric Walton in Rare Art Form
(God, E. Walton)
All songs and lyrics inspired by God
Songs and lyrics written, arranged, and performed by Eric Walton unless noted by *()

Heartfelt Dedication

The Opening Acknowledgement

Preface: Defining Moments

Overture I
*(Contains replayed sample from the book "Wisdom of Sirach Chapter 39 verses 1-16 (CPDV)")
Part I: The Wisdom of Eric Walton
1: Life
2: Progressive Growth
3: Valued Life
4: Assertive Will
5: Hope
6: Faith
7: Inspiration
8: Encouragement
9: Fulfillment
10: Achievement

Overture II
*(Contains replayed sample by Sir Henry Royce)
Part II: The Brilliance of Eric Walton
11: Splendid Tapestry Woven in Excellence

Overture III
*(Contains replayed sample by Vince Lombardi)
Part III: The Vision of Eric Walton
12: A Crying Heart Sees Crystal Clear

Epilogue: The Heart's Gratitude

The Closing Remark
*(Contains replayed sample by Carroll Bryant)

About The Author

Heartfelt Dedication

To you

To the greatness that you are

To the greatness that brings us together

The Opening Acknowledgement

God is the greatest...

Preface:
Defining Moments

These musings, proverbial in nature, are the result of God in His Greatness and Supreme Omnipotence directing and inspiring me over the course of time from October 2007 to the present and moreover my life. This is a collection of deliberation moments; contemplative, introspective, and reflective conversations with God as well as learned life lessons; formulating intuition, fueling my critical thinking and deductive reasoning. The ultimate desire which I seek throughout life is balance and satisfaction; this is my strive for perfection, albeit I went about this imperfectly and inefficiently.

I am one who always seeks answers for the sake of understanding, even seemingly to my detriment; my reasoning revolved around my imbalance and the needs to even the scales to balance everything. As my life came to the full head of peril, uncertainty, and void, I had to stop and realize who I am and why did I engage in particular actions and activities. I truly discovered myself to be pacified but never satisfied. Life was meaningless for many years with many days and nights rubbing dirt on the wound then walking if off; the pain would remain and only masked in stain. I had to discover the meaning of my life and my significance; in short, who I am and why I am meant to be.

Throughout this journey, God steered the drive inside of me to seek the essence; His essence. There were moments of trepidation due to uncertainty, unfamiliarity, and the unknown. There were moments when I was crippled, rendered useless, and ridiculed. There were moments when I secured answers only to lose security due to the ensuing questions. Circumstances provided worthy explanations yet seemed worthless. In hindsight, these were and continue to be instruments of insight; building intuition from introspection: the learned knowledge of and within myself and the gained understanding; all of which successfully creating, establishing, and honing a clearer mind and wiser kind.

This was and still remains an ongoing process, a continuous cycle if you will. Yes I stumble along this walk despite my constant improvement and refinement; however, the humble accept such and seek discipline and education from the stumble; welcoming God's correction in order to correct my errors, remaining humble throughout the process. Not only is this the way of the wise, this is for the sake of improving my efficiency and in essence achieving balance and satisfaction.

The answers that you seek are the answers of and within yourself. This is how we are created, this is our existence. For so long there has been a convoluted belief regarding seeking righteousness and spirituality; the result being hypocritical traditions leading to confusion, deception, false sense of entitlement, mental barriers and enslavement, and spiritual destruction; all of which is not of God and inefficient because of the mind and time being wasted.

God does not expect an imperfect person such as me to live a perfect life; rather He expects, more precise, He hopes and longs for an imperfect person to perfect the walk to achieve a divine destiny of greatness: the brilliance He establishes in the beginning by the excellence of wisdom.

That goes for you also, beloved.

This is the vision set before me and upon me.
This is my hope and the hope for you.
This is inspiration and you are my inspiration.

Overture I

A wise man will seek the wisdom of all the ancients, and he will be occupied in the prophets.

He will preserve the words of renowned men, and he will enter with them into the subtleties of parables.

He will search for the hidden meanings of proverbs, and he will become familiar with the mysteries of parables.

He will minister in the midst of great men, and he will appear in the sight of the foremost leader.

He will pass through the land of foreign nations. For he will test good and evil among men.

At first light, he will offer his heart with watchfulness to the Lord Who made him, and he will pray in the sight of the Most High.

He will open his mouth in prayer, and he will make supplication for his offenses.

For if the Lord is willing, He will fill him with the Spirit of understanding.

And he will send forth the eloquence of his wisdom like rain showers, and in his prayer, he will confess to the Lord.

And he will direct his counsel and his discipline, and he will meditate on his mysteries.

He will make the discipline of his doctrine clear, and he will glory in the law of the covenant of the Lord.

Many persons will together praise his wisdom, and it will never be abolished, for all ages.

The memory of him will not fade away, and his name will be sought from generation to generation.

The peoples will declare his wisdom, and the Church will announce his praise.

While he remains, he leaves behind a name greater than a thousand, and when he will rest, it will be to his benefit.

I will meditate further, so that I may explain. For I have been filled with a passion.

Part I:

The Wisdom of Eric Walton

Life

Section I

Knowledge is God. God is Knowledge.

Knowledge is the foundation, the very essence of life.

Without knowledge can there be existence. Without knowledge a being can exist.

God always exists and is always being; never a being or moment exists before or after, with or without God.

Therefore, beloved, upon deliberation, examination, and meditation, I behold and declare that knowledge is the root of life and is life being.

Section II

God's will brought forth the heavens, the earth, and the inhabitants of each; from merely a single idea, everything appeared here.

God, The Creator of all and The All-Knowing, brought forth man by His will, the Lord's will is by image, by earth, and by breath.

Thrice over is a human being filled with the Lord's essence naturally by design and by His will we are beings of knowledge: in image, in mold, and in spirit; as we were created last we are first, The Lord's will empowered and powered our will to name all that was created prior just as an infant knows the mother and father and states such; such words that the infant speaks are the first words proclaimed and spoken.

The knowledge that is God is the knowledge that created you, the knowledge instilled in you, and is that which you are and what you have always been.

Beloved, please know that your life is a marvel that transcends time. Your very being is the greatness of knowledge!

Section III

The Lord enlightens me to that which exists in me. I behold a light brighter than any.

The light is insight. This light illuminates from a mere thoughts, giving action and direction of the right path for growth and progression.

Knowledge is the clear light, the purest light, and the light that exists within; it is insightful.

Knowledge is a gift given by God. We are gifts created by God and of God; by God, we are gifted! Our presence is a culmination of presents here in the present; the gifts that we present, God willing, present the gift of life we are given, the gift that we indeed are.

This knowledge is a marvel to behold, and is worthy of praise. God being Supreme; revered for Who He is, His will, and all that He wills. We all exist from a thought; He wills us into existence merely from the knowledge that He is.

Knowledge is God. Knowledge is a gift. Acknowledge the gift of God.

Section IV

My perspective beholds knowledge as being powerful. The vastness of knowledge is life the existence of life, knowledge being responsible for all.

Therefore, knowledge is power.

Power is knowledge being and exuding. How else man was bestowed all dominion and power upon his creation when he was created last?

We are the images of God. We are the worth of such a distinct honor.

Indeed we are the worthy ones to be living and breathing beings of knowledge, the very knowledge that powers life! Literally we are living testaments of God!

Beloved, the extent of your knowledge is the power that you possess! Your capabilities are as your knowledge, your power is vast. The definition of your power is as your knowledge is defined.

Before God is none.

God is the Power Who has given you power.

God exists within you, is of your existence, and is why you exist.

Seek within yourself the very knowledge that you are and in doing so you seek your God given birthright which is glorious by nature. Seeking within self gives glory to God Who created you in His image; God giving you life and the power to progressively grow by nature.

Become knowledgeable of self and in doing so you become knowledgeable of God.

Section V

The knowledge is grounded. The power is humble. Knowledge is power and gratefulness.

Humility is set forth from the Power Who created you; as the Creator wields the power to make life, wielding the power to take life; rendering final judgment: God facilitates all existence of life
God is all knowledge and power; God is life, God wields life.
God willed into existence the heavens and earth, man and woman, and all that exists. God and His will exists and will always continue to exist regardless of all, everyone, and everything and if all, everyone, and everything does not exist.
God is the Answer, needs no answer, and needs never to answer to anyone; yet He answers those seeking Him and His answers are sufficient as well as humble.

With this in my heart, I can attest that fear is proper knowledge.

Fear is knowledge of God and is reverential.

Fear is the prosperous perspective of humility.

Fear is properly learning and measures learning properly.

Fear defines and enhances humilities; Knowledge begets fear.

Fear is power; Knowledge defines and enhances humilities.

We are of knowledge, power, and fear.

The fear of God is the knowledge of life, the power to be, and the just outcome if you choose to go against God.

Fear instills humility facilitate correction that is beneficial for seeking proper direction and staying on the right path and way.

Do what is right and fear going against God, beloved; such is how you shall receive all that you seek. This is the very means to grow by empowering yourself with the knowledge that is yours and that is you.

In my grounded and humble essence, I fear that I am deemed and rendered powerless by my Lord. My God bestows a gift upon me for His sake and will; for God created, formed, and gave me life. I seek God as the very desires and destinations I deem important. I pray that I obtain His mercy for all of my missteps and stumbles throughout my walk in life and obedience.

The fear of God is my splendid bliss.

Section VI

Knowledge is the peaceful heart, mind, and soul.

Knowledge sets forth peace.

Peace is a powerful state of being.

There exists a power in peace and peace comes with power; peace and power is one of the same.

God is the King of Peace; the Power by His will forms the galaxies and all within and this is an exertion of his peace in peace.

It is through God that I do have peace and I know God to be peace:
Who else guides me, sets me straight, and gives me rest throughout life?
Who else provides me the opportunity to grow from the knowledge that is my very being?

Beloved, discover and gain all that you are and exists within you.

To know is to grow.

This is peace in itself.

You are at the very peace existing within you and this makes you peace as from the creation in the beginning of time.

Knowledge is peace and peace is the hunger for knowledge; seeking the peaceful route is the quest in feeding this hunger.

Peace is gained in the fear of God, the knowledgeable mind, wielding the power of the favorable soul; God granting all the heart's desires.

This is God given opportunity and is exactly what God hopes and longs for us.

God facilitates such. God is such. God grants such to all.

Section VII

The treasure that God places within us is the knowledge that forms us, existing within us all. This wealth is indeed priceless; yet being priceless it grows in value, enhances value, and helps life to grow; its value comes in the ability to enhance. This treasure is sought and never found for it is not lost as God is never lost nor has knowledge ever left.

Peace of mind is glorious praise to God.

Beloved, I assure you that in God life exists and that knowledge is life itself.

Brilliance is one's knowledge and the resplendence of its glory.

Fear does not enslave. A lack of knowledge and proper perspective enslaves many of who are led astray and wondering aimlessly; ignorance being the oppression not making the slave free.

Knowing who you are and not knowing any direction is better than knowing a direction and not knowing yourself; such is the fine line between learning and surviving, being and doing.

Being the lead and being misled is a fine line between knowledge and ignorance.

One only has as much power given; however, ignorance renders one powerless and becoming under the power of anyone.

Fear is not a sign of weakness rather it is a sign of a strong soul; the one who shows no fear is the one who shows a false sense of strength lying in ignorance, this is truly weakness.

As you grow in stature and years, so should your knowledge; the storage space is increased and the capacity is capable of holding greater capacities.

The ignorant ones are never at peace. They do not know themselves, therefore not knowing of Whom they are.

You can never be as powerful as God. If you achieve one hundred years of life here on earth that still is merely ten percent of God's day. However, your one hundred years shall be a delightful offering to the Most High if He deems your brilliance being glorious.

Knowledge is wonderful, a marvel to behold, beloved. The same is said of God and all that He creates, especially those not dwelling in ignorance.

Progressive Growth

Section I

Without wisdom can one be wise.

The humble and wise shall indeed rise.

The rise is with wisdom.

Knowledge is breathing and wisdom is advancing; as I inhale and exhale, I excel and prevail.

Wisdom is the way to excel, the way of excellence, and the way to become excellent.

Wisdom promotes life and preserves life. It is the means to prevail. The wise shall always be preferred and prevalent.

The Word of God is wisdom for God's Word is wise and He is All-Wise.

God hands down wisdom.

The Messiah being One of Word, the perfect embodiment of Word; Jesus, being the Messiah and the coming forth of perfection in wisdom, came in and of the Word of God.

Jesus, being perfect of Word embodied, ascended on high; wisdom being paramount for His ascension to the highest of heights; His name being everlasting with wisdom and in His every step, growing greater with each breath and step; the perfect embodiment and personification of sheer brilliance and superior excellence throughout His life.

Every breath in the rarefied air of wisdom excels and prevails in and to the higher heights; therefore, wisdom is progressive growth, a love like none other and one to always desire and embrace.

I seek the love, holding my head high above seeking wisdom. Wisdom is never lost or found for I receive this love as I seek. Wisdom is the lovely art that locates the treasure deep within my soul.

Wisdom is a never failing guiding light that is impervious to darkness. Wisdom is the light set forth: the love validating fear's reverence, the strength resonating from peace, the perseverance coming forth from power; all of which are the natural progression of life and the means of advancement and ascensions through life.

The rise comes upon me and all who seek to embrace love; wisdom being the precious jewel, a love near and dear to the humble and wise and their heart's desire.

Section II

Strength exudes from peace.

Perseverance exists from power.

Fear is a sign of wisdom at work.

The wise are at peace.

Love is the appreciation of life.

Wisdom is the strength to love and persevere.

Love is wisdom.

Perseverance is strength.

To love is to persevere.

To be wise is to be strong.

The one who gives wisdom is the one who loves; God gave Jesus, a Symbol of His love for all. The Messiah gave Himself to all for all. God gave his Word promising all who received His Word life, this taking love, perseverance, and strength; this being love, perseverance, and strength. He is as He says, He does as I shall.

Wisdom is unconditional, transcending any condition and time.

Wisdom conditions decisions, bearing fruit for a condition to come to fruition.

Water and sunlight facilitates growth of the planted seed. Wisdom facilitates growth of the human being planted in right; both growing progressively and gaining value as nature runs course.

Wisdom is maturity and security; securing timeless growth and maturity as time progresses.

Wisdom is progressive growth.

Being wise has its advantages, beloved.

Valued Life

Section I

Knowledge is the borne fruit.

Wisdom is the ripening of the borne fruit.

Understanding is the fruit ripened in its prime and at its best.

Understanding rests in wisdom.

Understanding is the rest gained from wisdom.

Beloved, please heed wisdom for it is the key to understanding the knowledge that is you, is you, and is life.

Understanding makes knowledge crystal clear.

A precious crystal holds value that grows more in value with maturity and time, the result being the flawless shine of priceless value and splendor; the gratitude of the love discovered and embraced.

Section II

Understanding is the relaxation to the heart, mind, and soul.

Understanding is the state of grace that gives comfort and confidence to state grace gracefully.

Understanding commands respect and respectfully commands.

Understanding is the key to opening doors and key for all thereafter as well as key to the Hereafter, this life is the understanding of a forever being discovered.

Understanding is the meal prepared by wisdom from the ingredients of knowledge.

The fruits of knowledge are taken by wisdom bearing into fruition fruitfulness that which is understanding.

Respect is due to the one who loves and perseveres despite a condition, situation, or reciprocation.

There is a confidence and comfort as well as a confidence in the comfort that rests in strength; the comfort through strength, the respect and illumination of love: this being the confirmation of fruition, none being in vain.

Results validate actions and in turn actions validate results; the value is set wherefrom and reached therein.

The process to grow from rest to gain rest is a cycle of completion always to be completed.

The value of life is continuous to increase value and upkeep value.

Understanding is the reward earned from wisdom: The Word rewards the Holy Spirit, a Spirit of understanding, to the believers who seek to embrace love, love being wisdom. The humble and wise receives the ultimate Comforter and Helper in reception of the Spirit, such being a priceless reward increasing and upholding the life fully valued.

Section III

Beloved, I beckon and beseech you to embrace wisdom as the caring and loving friend whose desire is to love and embrace you. The benefits of wisdom enable growth and a progressive lifestyle which is paramount for a fully valued life; understanding being crystal clear.

Understanding illuminates the peaceful route, this being the right path and the right way; opening eyes to a greater light, love, and splendor. This key when it comes to recognizing a bigger picture and a greater way of life to be attained.

The painter has a vision upon gazing the canvas, seeing the picture before it fully develops and not knowing how it shall develop fully, all from a distance. The one who sees crystal clear with understanding and values life naturally sees forward and recognizes the Vision of God!

Assertive Will

Section I

God is of everything. God is everything. God sees everything.

The open ear to wisdom is of the humble and wise. The closed ear to wisdom is of the foolish and prideful; free will is given to both.

Free will is way of a cloud envisioned or a clouded vision: one being full of value, the other not valuing life in full; yet life exists as God exists for God is life.

God gives the living being free will as He envisioned from the creation in the beginning. The one with assertive will is the one who gives way to the Vision of God, seeing beyond self; seeing as one seeking God in the beginning: everything of God, God, and everything God sees. God is the center of life and everything seen in life.

The one who values life is the one who views freedom as a blessing of God; this one is a cultured mind belonging to a culture of those alike in mind, assertive in light of God, seeing crystal clear in the proper understanding. The one viewing freedom as one's own doing does not truly understand, thus is one that does not truly value life and is living a lie.

The understanding ones see the light ahead, recognizing God and asserting to realize God willingly. The misunderstanding ones sit in a selfish spotlight of self-revelry; this being the difference between glory and fame respectively.

Beloved, see the better tomorrow and understand there is nothing worse than not having a yesterday. Understanding the past in the present is a gift; appreciation, gratitude, and thankfulness in this presents you a future. This is the understanding of the pure and unconditional love given to you and that which is for you.

The culture marches in tune synchronized to the Vision of God and thus are set free; seeing is hearing by an unspoken Word. Conversely, the ones lacking culture are slaves to rhythms to the beat of their own drums.

Those among the cultured hear the same tune differently but still march in unison in recognition of God, Word of God, and Vision of God.

God is omnipotence, the center of everything.

God is of everything. God is everything. God sees everything.

Section II

The one blissful in ignorance,
The one sorrowful in wisdom,
Both do not recognize God.
Both do not understand God in heart, mind, and soul.

The rapport of the cultured is the Lord's calling,
These are the one who speak when God speaks to them.

Recognize God when he calls and speaks, beloved.

Hope

The Vision of God is realized by me.

I realize the Lord in creating me hopes that I set forth from Him
To grow and mature,
To assert and envision myself,
In hope that I return to Him

I have returned from whence I came in hope of gaining and increasing value.
I have the hope of reaching God, coming to, and grasping for God Who wills me;
Decreasing myself with humility and obedience which my heart desires,
My mind understands and soul values.

The Lord's calling resonates within my essence.
I answer by my assertive will in hope of realizing Him
I bask in His glory.
I settle for satisfaction in Him.
My meaningful life is a full circle, graceful and powerful which God is merciful and powerful;
A cycle of the Power empowering and powering me,
I shall remain powerful in him.

This is Creation.
This is for knowledge
Created in image, mold, and spirit

Lord, as a reflection of you,
This illumination of my resplendence is a glory in praise and worship in total reverence of You, O Lord!
The power from whence I come to where I arrive is a delightful praise,
A splendid state of mind
My splendor is a reflection and testament of You, Lord!
I am the hope that I long,
In You I seek me and in me I seek You.
Lord, my spirit grows and replenishes,
The Spirit of the Lord is refreshing

Give me an inclination worthy of You, O Lord, by way of Your will.
Set forth in me to believe, to move outward and, and to strive in the honor of Your will for You choose me to be an inspiration.
I pray my life is strengthened to do Your will as You set upon me.
Your will upholds me, accomplishing Your will uplifts me.

Lord, I appreciate the love You give me.
For me to fulfill Your will and show Your glory is humbling and mesmerizing,
A testament of brilliance;
By the excellence of Your name I testify.

Amen.

Faith

Section I

The Lord's will brings the hope to believe in Him:
From this belief to emigrate in trust of Him,
From this emigration to strive to Him,

In such a progression, talents begets tithe.

God rewards the just who pay in talents:
The talent is faith in the Lord's will
The emigration is the focus on the Lord's will
The strive is the determination in the Lord's will

The focus and determination is the applied talent;
The resulting work of faith is justifiably redeemed.
The passion is the full payment of tithe redeemed by progressing in and with talent.
The passion and its splendor are justified
The passion is inspiring.
The passionate is an inspiration.

To struggle is to seek God's favor,
Such is graceful and merciful.
To reach the goal of the struggle is to receive God's favor.
To seek and to receive is the inspirational art of the talented,
Splendid, justified, and beautiful in God's sight

Section II

In failure rests the abundance of success;
The successful who credits self is truly a failure.
God's mercy offers success:
The understanding gained from the wisdom of God's mercy is success for all who fail;
And in that redemption rests a glorious success and heavenly source of inspiration.

The one who accepts the Lord's will is hopeful,
The one who rejects the Lord's will is hopeless;
The Lord's will being greater than one's assertive will, as He is the greatest.

The wind upholds the dove weary in flight,
Yet the dove still must lift just a single wing to be held high;
God upholds and uplifts the determined;
The just are held high;
The weary always being made to rise above to inspire all.

Inspiration

The Lord justifies me an inspiration
The inspired motivates by Word set forth to accomplish Word
The inspired testimony motivates the accomplished
I inspire the just to set forth by the Lord's inspiration
The Lord inspires me to do His work, motivating me His chosen to accomplish His Word

The Lord is my strength and is Who strengthens me, the inspiration a gift of strength;
The inspired minds chosen to be abound in strength:
How else is it possible to be motivated; enduring the weight of the Word, the Word creating the world and everything else?
How else can the inspired carry the world's weight on shoulders and not be crushed?

The strong sees the joy in the journey crystal clear and stays the course
The reward of an accomplished inspiration is the renaissance,
The renaissance is an accomplishment abound in strength

The Lord chose me; my passion is a result of His calling:
My ears hear His call
My eyes behold His splendor,
My heart, mind, and soul moves out and strives in my talents, the resplendence of His glory:
Why would I not be motivated to accomplish what God has chosen?
Why would I not be inspiration to motivate those to seek greatness they see accomplished before them?

As I am inspiration, I am an inspired accomplishment!

The inspired shall be of the Lord's strength;
He inspired by Word He sets upon His chosen:
The chosen outweighs the called;
An inspiration strengthens the masses;
The strength in the numbered builds strength in numbers.
The Word is heavy:
The Word is easily carried by the motivated chosen.
The Word is easier to carry by those called and delivered to lift an inspiration.
The called lifts up hands for the chosen; the accomplishment is deliverance.
The burden of the Word weighs more to the chosen who carries forward for others' deliverance than those called to receive deliverance which they seek.

The glory of God is in sight of all; all ranked and thereby bestowed talents accordingly by and for God's glory.

Inspiration begets inspiration.

Encouragement

Accomplishment begets encouragement and is one of the same.

Accomplishing a goal sets forth an abundance of strength and renews strength.

The better tomorrow being granted in the form of a new day seen, a renaissance borne into fruition

From a renewed life comes a day reborn;
A seed of inspiration planted to bear new fruit,
The harvest abundant and plentiful:
Why would one bear fruit if not to feed the brethren?
Why would the inspired bear nourishment if those seeking such for replenishment of their bodies could not attain this very sustenance?
Would inspiration not go forth, being sent forth and inspired by God to motivate, to supply a vision of a renewed life for those to seize the victory of a new day; bringing glory to God and a glorious resplendence?

Beloved, the encouraged are the strength of God

A vision of inspiration in movement is a vision of a purposeful life.
An inspiration is a Vision of God
An inspirational wondrous work of sublime hope and strength
A splendid achievement

The victory in the accomplishment is the supreme strengthening of the heart, mind, and soul
The encouraged are not one with the losers

As the sun rises for the benefit of sight
And the promotion of a new day,
The inspiration gives opportunity to behold;
The opportunity to bear witness to a new day,
Reinvigoration and renaissance,
The inspiration for a better tomorrow

Fulfillment

The enlightened ones are those who are fulfilled and have fulfilled,
A shining light of encouragement;
The rays of inspiration, nourishing and replenishing,
Establishing the brilliance of the inspiration and the inspired,
The encouragement and the encouraged;
These being a highest of heights achieved and reached,
A cycle reflective as the sun is upon the still waters

The gardener cultivates the garden accordingly
As natures dictates
Until the garden fulfills conditions of bearing crops
Bearing crops at the behest of those with desires and needs.
The garden produces;
The garden provides;
The garden thereafter is cultivated yet again to fulfill the condition to bear crops again
As nature dictates
The garden and the gardener are paramount:
One's success is of the other;
Both are inspired by God's hope and will.
The hope to replenish and the will to nourish;
Both flourish for one another, from one another,
Both fulfill desires and needs,
Both are of God and inspired by God.

The fulfillment of the Lord's will is one with the winners.
Fulfillment is fruitful;
Bearing the fruit for the harvest, the appointed season
Fulfillment is sharing.

The Lord establishes His hope and will in the beginning:
The hope and will to grow forth
From a tree of knowledge
To a ray of hope;
Becoming of God and coming of age;
A light for the hoping,
A tool for the learning,
A drink of water for the parched soul thirsty for righteousness,
Food for thought for the starved mind hungry for knowledge;
All for the greater good,
All to see the better tomorrow

Beloved, this is winning the life and love that God set forth at life:
The full brilliance of life, knowledge, and God and all His excellence
The full brilliance of your life and the excellence it conveys

Achievement

Section I

The rise comes upon me.
The humble and wise shall indeed rise,
The rise comes upon me;
Feeding the brethren who craves wisdom,
The rise comes upon me;
Quenching the thirst with a cup runneth over,
The rise comes upon me;
The rarefied airs,
The rise comes upon me;
The celestial views,
The rise comes upon me;
Basking in the glory of sheer brilliance by superior excellence,
The rise comes upon me;
The euphoria of the victory seized,
The rise comes upon me;
The splendid achievement,
The rise comes upon me;
The refreshing satisfaction,
The rise comes upon me;
The justified reward for a beautiful struggle,
The rise comes upon me;
The feeling of accomplishment,
The rise comes upon me.

Section II

The shining brilliance of the enlightened mind,
The rise comes upon me;
The countenance of the inspired immersed in excellence,
The rise comes upon me;
The highest heights,
The rise comes upon me;
The best hope,
The rise comes upon me;
The sublime peace,
The rise comes upon me;
The supreme splendor,
The rise comes upon me;
The superior excellence,
The rise comes upon me;
The meaningful life,
The rise comes upon me;
Living a life full of passion and purpose driven,

The rise comes upon me;
The fruitful, fulfilling, and winning,
The rise comes upon me.

Section III

Achievement is never the beginning of the end
It is completing a beginning;
When you complete a beginning you come full circle;
Achieving a divine cycle, a splendid achievement of supreme brilliance and excellence:
You appreciate it
You give the glory
You bask in the moment
You stay humble and hungry
You never forget the past
You come full circle, constantly learning and living and not memorizing and surviving

Achievement is a completion of life, beloved
The knowledge that begins life, is life, and completes life:
When one exists is there knowledge of one's existence?
When one no longer exists does not the knowledge of one's existence remain?

Therefore, beloved, knowledge never ceases as God never ceases
For God is knowledge and God is life
God remains and the knowledge of you shall remain.

So achieve all that you truly can, beloved:
Truly live and learn,
Engage and acquire,
Evolve and fulfill,
In all that you do, in all that you desire
For yourself, for your brethren, and most assuredly for God
For this is happiness and happiness is the best success
For God created you in image, mold, and spirit;
For God loves us
For God is the best and greatest
For God wants our best and greatest in glory of Him

The Lord elevates me to the highest heights; He gives me the most sublime refreshment of excellence for my brilliance
God is my balance:
He holds me upright; His Almighty, All-Powerful hand uplifts me
Through Him I am wise, for Him I am humble, by Him I endure
Of Him I am, with Him I rise above

The rise comes upon me

Overture II

Strive for perfection in everything you do. Take the best that exists and make it better. When it does not exist, design it.

Part II:

The Brilliance of Eric Walton

Splendid Tapestry Woven in Excellence

(1) Life	**(2) Progressive Growth**	**(3) Valued Life**
God	Jesus (Messiah)	Holy Spirit
Knowledge	Wisdom	Understanding
Power	Perseverance	Confidence
Fear	Love	Respect
Peace	Strength	Comfort

Life → Progressive Growth → Valued Life

- *Vision of God recognized*

(4) Assertive Will

Valued Life → Assertive Will → Hope

- *Vision of God realized*

(5) Hope

- *The Lord's calling*

Hope → The Lord's will → Believe

(6) Faith

Believe (Faith) → Emigrate (Focus) → Strive (Determination)

- *Passion (Justified Faith)*

(7) Inspiration

- *Purpose*

Inspiration → Motivation → Accomplishment

(8) Encouragement

Encouragement → Enlightenment → Fulfillment

(9) Fulfillment

(10) Achievement

Overture III

Perfection is not attainable, but if we chase perfection we can catch excellence.

Part III:

The Vision of Eric Walton

A Crying Heart Sees Crystal Clear

This is the result of a desire and vision; an artful achievement in balance and efficiency. This is the culmination of commonalities within different perspectives, yet the discipline remained the same; bridging the gap and removing hindrances and limitations that existed over time, the true essence and meaning and purpose of the power of self-awareness and spirituality: the divine need to love and grow, live and learn, and the appreciation and seeking of the heart's desires. We all deserve happiness and love but never do we deserve to be done unjustly for the sake of another's happiness. We all have a God given right to know who we are and what our worth is; not having that devalued and diminished by the deceitful and self-serving.

This is an ideology to best serve the walk of life, the strive for perfection. This is the encouragement and enlightenment to fulfill dreams and visions. This is a breath of fresh air; a testament that the only restrictions which exists are ignorance and misunderstanding, both of which being removed with the brilliance of knowledge and the excellence of wisdom. This is for the hopeless and the weary, young and old. This is food for the soul. This is the musical art of thought playing to calm and relax my heart, mind, and soul; seeing the hope for a new day crystal clear, advancing from the hard earned yesterday with a love gained that keeps giving and growing.

So many days and nights I sought relief from the crying heart; the tears for myself and the world, both in a steady and deep decline. It seemed that I was running in place wasting time with nowhere to go: The more that I gained, the less I was satisfied. My life meant nothing and served no purpose. I always felt obligated to help others; however, it served no purpose for I lacked the true meaning of myself, imbalance and inefficiency to the maximum. For that reason alone, I realized therein rests the need for a new perspective to be brought forth and developed; one that is not restrictive, does not discredit any epiphany gained, and free of hypocrisy.

This is my splendid state of mind; the new and rare jewel, a gift that I personally longed and hoped to achieve and gain and this new number system being Splendid Mathematics. This is what I deliver to the world for the world; this is what I shall leave the world, and God willing, shall be the transcendence I leave behind long after I ascend. This is a legacy as much as a look into the windows of my mind; a constant elevation and evolution and dynamic culmination, honing the gift that God gives me. This is my desire to be great and to provide greatness; all for appreciation and love of greatness, the sheer brilliance of knowledge and the superior excellence of wisdom. And this was all searching for a love I had long ago never went away, for love is forever.

This is my strive for perfection. This is my satisfaction. This is from me to you; for love and from love. Life comes in threes and love is right there. Live life.

Peace.

Epilogue:
The Heart's Gratitude

Though this is a soliloquy in streams of consciousness, this is a love letter written in album form, a song within songs never sang but forever playing. The gratitude that I have for wisdom is immeasurable for wisdom is a love gained. Truthfully I cannot love myself if I do not share a love such as this willingly or unwillingly; love is the answer, fulfilling desires and prophecies alike, and achieving destiny.

During the crafting, developing, and honing of this art which is me and my musings, different people came to my mind all throughout this evolving process; some more than others. It was in this when I realized that my original hope and intent was surpassed; God took my heart's desire seeing a more prosperous and sublime achievement per His will, achieving His glory for me and by me; fulfilling my heart's desire benefits not only me but the greater good, the opportunity to fulfill prophecy and manifest destiny. As I basked in the moment of this divine revelation, I became wise to this fact and grew stronger that my musings speak to the behalf of a personal relationship just as God has a personal relationship with every single one of us; a relationship with a love shared not only is beneficial to that particular individual, it is beneficial to all of a like heart, mind, and spirit seeking the same to embrace.

The more I mused, the more I realized the distinct desire and hope within myself. The more written, the more a particular dynamic with a dear friend of mine slowly becoming part of my written words, ultimately fulfilling and strengthening a relationship long lost over what almost is two decades; conforming and revealing the phenomenon of a timeless treasured friendship, an answered call in truth. Despite this fact and the many accompanying regrets over time, it is as if we have never been separated; the chemistry and energy is supreme, a marvelous phenomenon in itself and a glorious shining light. The sheer brilliance in completing one another in thought and excellence is the shared desire fulfilled with true friends reclaimed; the love for a dear friend is the renaissance, the new day is the refined renewal of life. Although contact has been reestablished, there still always awaits the opportunity to embrace. In essence, this friend solely evolved into the muse of this art; as an artist has one for inspiration of a painting, an album, a song, etc. This is how one must seek the love of a new day and the hope of a better tomorrow; ultimately with the fulfilling of gaining the satisfaction desired and long sought the very completion of a life cycle and gained successes.

The best analogy of this dynamic and its transcendence, much like this art form, is this: I lost hold of a jewel in her. The rarity of the jewel always existed. My value of the jewel grew as the hope to reclaim the jewel as time grew longer apart. Although my hope dwindled and was supplanted with regret and sorrow, my knowledge of the jewel is the value I would cherish; desiring to receive and reclaim the jewel one day God willing. Despite not being in my grasp, the jewel accumulates and maintains value naturally; if others come across her or not; whether others truly value her or truly know her worth, my value of her never diminishes as time passes and slips away. Time passes, life progresses, and at the appointed season which is truly unexpected and only known by God, I discover her by an inspired movement. The time apart is forgotten; the time reunited is euphoria.

To this dear and lovely friend I forever am grateful; my heart's gratitude abundantly joyful; a recognition of God and His ways. Our dynamic fulfilling all that I have pondered and scripted in my desires, hopes, and visions; all of which God inspires, sending me forth to achieve. I desired to convey my thought process and personal testament of my gift from God and in doing so, have gained way more than I have ever expected. Despite our time apart, you balance and complete me as a missing link; understanding me sincerely and being that energetic dose that I needed to push forward. The time away matters not as long as I have it in my being to seek you as I do for God, for the love of God is transcendent, love is transcendent as it is excellent.

Love is a beautiful thing and wisdom is a love worth sharing. The satisfaction of the heart's desire shall not settle for anything less.

The Closing Remark

I strive for perfection – I settle for satisfaction.

About the Author

Eric Walton was born on February 4, 1977 to his parents Robin Walton (nee DeNeal) and James Walton in Gary, IN, specifically hailing from the section known as Aetna; this neighborhood being where he learned a lot of life lessons, gained confidence and positive reinforcement from many friends, family members, and peers of various backgrounds and walks of life.

He graduated from William A. Wirt High School in 1995 and Purdue University in 2000.

Despite being a graduate of Purdue, he considers himself more a student of the art of life and life itself with the hopes that one day he shall achieve a legacy and level of timeless recognition; more important than that, finally achieve the happiness he so hopes and longs.

Eric has one sibling, Anthony Walton.

He has one daughter, Erica Walton, who is resting in peace for she was stillborn on January 19, 2013.

Thank You

www.ingramcontent.com/pod-product-compliance
Lightning Source LLC
Chambersburg PA
CBHW081741170526
45167CB00009B/3895